John Kingston James

Daydreams

to which are added some translations from the Italian

John Kingston James

Daydreams
to which are added some translations from the Italian

ISBN/EAN: 9783741161025

Manufactured in Europe, USA, Canada, Australia, Japa

Cover: Foto ©Thomas Meinert / pixelio.de

Manufactured and distributed by brebook publishing software
(www.brebook.com)

John Kingston James

Daydreams

DAY DREAMS,

TO WHICH ARE ADDED SOME TRANSLATIONS

FROM THE ITALIAN.

BY

SIR JOHN KINGSTON JAMES, Baronet, M.A.

CORRESPONDING MEMBER OF THE ROYAL ACADEMY
DELLA CRUSCA.

Author of a Translation of Tasso's "Gerusalemme Liberata."

" She was my vision in the night,
My waking dream by day."
Old Song, 1607.

LONDON:
PRINTED FOR PRIVATE CIRCULATION.
1879.

TO

THE ARCH-CONSUL AND MEMBERS OF
THE ROYAL ACADEMY
DELLA CRUSCA.

TO YOU I DEDICATE THESE LEAVES, AS EARNEST OF

THE DEEP AND ABIDING SENSE OF THE

GREAT HONOUR CONFERRED, IN ELECTING ME

A MEMBER OF YOUR ILLUSTRIOUS

BODY.

J. K. J.

CONTENTS.

b

x   *Contents.*

TRANSLATIONS.

Contents.

Contents.

TO THE ARCH-CONSUL AND MEMBERS
OF THE ROYAL ACADEMY
DELLA CRUSCA

ON BEING NOMINATED A CORRESPONDING MEMBER.

SCARCE had I hoped that in my
waning years,
When every fenfe is burden'd with
their weight,
I fhould experience a new pleafure—I
That had exhaufted all the old—youth, health,
Arms, idlenefs, ev'n every hope, fave the one,
And foreign travel, and the arch delight
Of telling in our tongue an alien's thoughts.
Ev'n this, the mafter paffion of my prime,

B

Began fomewhat to pall, although, at times,
When mufing o'er the great original,
All its old charm came back as vividly
As when at firft beneath its fpell I choked.
From faireft bower I pafs once more to field,
Where the horrible, harmonious trumpet rings,
Then back from all its carnage and its din
To the fweet, filent folitudes of love.
Now feems the poem on a rofe leaf writ,
Now on a fhield amid the fume of war.
Happy, thrice happy, do I deem the choice
That led me to explore its boundlefs wealth,
Inftead of baring my own poverty !
But ftill the poet ever feem'd a ftar
Whom I could neither grafp nor realize,
He loom'd fo diftant, ftately, and fublime;
When, of a fudden, all amazed, I ftart
To find that as 'twixt heaven and earth we
      meet.
But can all this be true ?—or, do I dream,
And wake to find life's dream reality—
Now that all former pleafures are eclipfed,

Hearing my humble felf in the fame breath
Named with Torquato Taffo—and by You!
And that your great Academy has deign'd
In me to honour the illuftrious dead.
But no; I cannot ev'n in thought allow
Myfelf to arrogate fuch honour—nay,
Rather would I his mighty fhade invoke,
And in the midft of you who know him beft,
His pardon afk that, having dared fo much,
I had not better reprefented him;
Having fail'd to follow his tranfcendent flight,
Or catch the infpiration of his mufe,
Nor gave my country but a baftard found
Of his harmonious and majeftic verfe,
Which after lapfe of ages echoes ftill,
And with as grand fonorous mufic rings,
As when he firft in his full vigour fang.
But haply, if long ftudy and great love
Of my great mafter may excufe defects,
I fhall not feek forgivenefs all in vain,
Affured of your indulgent fympathy,
Who in my poor attempt have recognized

An honeft wifh to extend Italian fame,
And whofe approval is, I feel, a fpur
To roufe me to frefh efforts, and at leaft,
By them my utter gratitude to fhow.
Not kings, though they the fount of honour
      deem'd,
Could have beftow'd an honour half fo prized
As that which from your hands I now receive
And, as firftfruits, I crave the privilege
To atone with him[1] whofe loving care has
      raifed
A living monument to Taffo's fame,
And on it place, in kindred fympathy,
The wreath your favour has accorded me,
But which fits ill upon my blufhing brow.
So for the future may a common love
Your members bind, conftraining them to cry
With one accord, and with a fingle voice,
"Onorate l' altiffimo poeta!"
And fo efface the undefervèd ftains
Upon him caft by fons of yours of yore.

  [1] Signor Cefare Guafti, Secretary of the Academy.

Thus were rewarded the long years of toil,
Thus crown'd the aspirations of a life!
Thus could I vaunt at least reflected fame,
If link'd with Tasso's my unworthy name.

TO GARIBALDI.

MILAN, OCTOBER, 1860.

NCE more I pass Alps' icy chains,
And feel already in my veins
   The blood more light and free;
Into new life it seems to leap
As I descend thy mountains steep—
   Enchanting Italy!

Here pregnant earth and nature teem
With rank exuberance, they seem
   Unlike our latitudes;
The very grape upon the vine,
As if anticipating wine,
   Its amber juice exudes.

And what rich contrafts ftrike the eye!
Oleanders 'gainft yon azure fky,
 In crimfon drifts behold.
What lovely tints, what mellow tones,
The purple figs, the very ftones
 Here lichen'd into gold!

Again I hear the glowing tongue
That Petrarch, Taffo, Dante, fung;
 To me, its fimple found
Appears more fweet than all the fenfe,
Than all the wit or eloquence
 In other language found.

But Hark! who doth his thunders
   launch,
Collecting as an avalanche
 Frefh force from every fide?
Who, rolling onwards gathers ftrength
From kindred fouls, aroufed at length,
 Their joy, their hope, their pride!

Who came, faw, conquer'd—nay, whofe
    name
Won bloodlefs victories ere he came—
    Whofe fhadow fcared away
The ruffian hordes whom tyrant power
Had bribed with gold—but in the hour
    Of danger, where were they?

They could not fave the Bourbon's throne
From one who bearded them alone,
    And did a realm o'erthrow :
Who won their hireling ranks and took
St. Elmo's fortrefs by a look,
    Nor ftruck a fecond blow.

Since faith of all his powers was chief,
He paufed not to believe belief,
    But haften'd to the goal.
Self-truft, the child of fimple faith,
Our ftay in life, our hope in death,
    So utterly fill'd his foul.

To Garibaldi. 9

Like noxious vapours, which the fun
Difpels, by fimply fhining on,
  So at his mere advance
The King fled howling in difmay,
The motley hofts diffolved away
  At Garibaldi's glance.

To thee and to thy loyal King
The inebriate people pæans fing
  From rife to fet of fun;
On Milan's dome the fnowy fpires
Blaze with the light of thoufand fires
  That tell of freedom won.

And foon there will be heard no
      more
From Venice to Sicilia's fhore
  The Goth's barbaric twang;
But in its place will ring the "Si"
Of one united Italy,
  As Dante dream'd and fang.

c

But though Utopian fophifts wrote,
With giant force thy right hand fmote—
  And fo broke through the charm.
The poet's hope, the patriot's fcheme,
Had ftill remain'd an idle dream
  Without thy trenchant arm.

Hence unborn ages will not fail
Thee, Garibaldi, yet to hail
  As the moft glorious fon
Of that fair land thy arm did free
From torture, chains, and flavery,
  Thou fecond Wafhington!

Thee we fhall fee, the conteft o'er,
Thy fabre fheath'd, retire once more
  To lone Caprera's ifle;
Defpifing earth's moft fought-for ranks,
Content to read thy country's thanks
  In her awaken'd fmile.

"He who does not imagine in ſtronger and better lineaments, and in ſtronger and better light than his periſhing mortal eye can ſee, does not imagine at all."—BLAKE.

OFT at the hour when day is breaking,
    ing,
  Between a-ſleeping and awaking,
    I ſee with ſtill-cloſed eyes
Bright viſions, ſo intenſely bright
That, melting with exceſs of light,
    They vaniſh as they riſe.

Glimpſes of golden lands I ſnatch,
Strains of unearthly muſic catch,
  Borne on whoſe lofty flight
I ſpurn the earth, and as I riſe
To heaven, it ſeems the opening ſkies
    My raviſh'd ſoul invite.

Into the meafurelefs expanfe
Of peopled planets I advance,
   Where Jupiter and Mars,
And Mercury and many more,
Though of the brighteft, pale before
   The illimitable ftars.

And higher, higher, ever on,
Far paft the regions of the fun,
   The ecftatic fpirit fprings
To new and ever-brightening fpheres,
Whofe mufic in my fpell-bound ears
   With found feraphic rings ;

And thinks, as all entranced it roams,
" Thefe ftars, it muft be, are the homes
   Of mortals after death—
The many manfions which the Lord
In His reveal'd life-giving Word
   To mankind promifeth."

Tranfported by fuch thoughts, I find
Two powers contending in the mind
   Which fdeigning the control
Of confcioufnefs to bind it, feels
A fomething that unconfcious fteals
   Upon the hidden foul.

A fomething which we can't define,
But which, lefs human than divine,
   Unlocks the fecret fprings
Of a myfterious latent fenfe
That tells of future providence,
   And of forgotten things.

The ghofts of fcarce-remember'd years,
And fhadowy forms and fhadowy fears,
   Of joys for ever fled,
Of hope that drooping oft revives,
Of faith that unextinguifh'd lives,
   Though hope itfelf be dead.

And indefinable fenfations,
Vague yearnings, ftruggles, afpirations—
   A doubtful fecond fight
That can but dimly, blindly fee,
Till quicken'd from its lethargy,
   By more than mortal light.

And fhe, my darling upon earth,
Transfigured through the fecond birth,
   In radiant youth is there;
But much more beautiful fhe feems
Than ever in my wildeft dreams
   I had imagined her.

Her hair floats on her neck, her eyes
Have caught frefh meaning from the
      fkies,
   And all beatified
An angel fhe before me ftands,
And beckoning with uplifted hands,
   Invites me to her fide.

Do I waking think, or fleeping dream?
As things paft comprehenfion feem
  My 'wilder'd thoughts to ftrain,
And in their wanderings to have
     caught
A fpark beyond the pale of thought
  That penetrates the brain,

Which inform'd with tranfcendent light
Revels in riotous delight
  To fober fenfe unknown,
Making of all that fcience knows,
Of all that fancy can difclofe,
  An empire of its own.

By fuch celeftial virtue fired,
Columbus faw, as if infpired,
  Another world, whence he,
In full-plumed faith his fails unfurl'd,
And reach'd that undifcover'd world
  Acrofs an uncrofs'd fea.

So we may in this mortal ftrife
Trace fhadows of that other life,
   For man by Jefus won,
But which, as will'd by Supreme will,
We fhall not fully fee until
   Our earthly race is run.

The fhipwreck'd failor in his hour
Of extreme peril feels a power—
   A fpell—a know not what,
Which at the moment ere he finks
Welds in one lengthen'd chain the
      links
   Of time and place forgot.

And as beneath the water yawns,
Before his fight a future dawns
   Of mingled doubt and dread;
A memory for life entomb'd
Is in that awful hour exhumed;
   The grave gives back its dead.

As thus the darkneſs, touch'd with light,
Lays open to his ſtartled ſight
  The long arrears of ſin;
Like one exploring haunted halls,
Whom ſudden ſpeſtral fright appals,
  He dares not look within.

For who will venture to gainſay,
When at the laſt doom-dealing day
  Our God our Judge we ſee,
That His dread record of the ſoul,
Be not the everlaſting roll
  Of tell-tale memory?

But, thank'd be God! in child-like faith
We can deride the power of death,
  Through Chriſt's atonement free,
And with the inſpired apoſtle ſing
Triumphant, "Where is, death, thy ſting?
  Where, grave, thy viſtory?"

D

TRANSLATING TASSO

ON THE BANKS OF THE AWBEG—
SPENSER'S MULLA.

NTRANCED for hours by Mulla's
  ſtream I ſit,
  And on the page that once taught
    Spenſer pore;
For he drank deep of Taſſo's muſe; from it
 He drew his love of legendary lore.

Thus both his founts of inſpiration I
 Have at command—the river and the book,
While in my lap Torquato's volumes lie,
 Beneath my feet ſtill rolls the immortal brook.

Here where the beeches overarch its ſtream,
    And with their ſhade conceal day's gariſh
       light,
Rapt in a world of waking thought I dream :
    Nor idly wait return of ſlow-paced night.

My ſole diſtraction now—ah ! bliſsful eaſe—
    Is from their haunts to lure the golden trout,
Where curls the water with propitious breeze,
    And drag with zeſt my little victims out.

Hiſtoric Mulla ! like thy living ſtream
    May my undying numbers glide along,
And with like ſtrength and like tranſparence
      teem,
    The flowing tide of my harmonious ſong.

And while purſuing its uncheck'd career,
    Still varying beauties like thyſelf unfold ;
There ſtealing gently—daſhing madly here,
    Deep, yet not tame, though ſparkling ſtill
     not cold.

Now genial May with violets gems the banks,
  And the fward robes in fuit of brighteft
    green ;
With wild wood-forrel pregnant Nature pranks
  The fpot ftill haunted by a Faery Queen.

Not from bald fancy had the poet fought
  His infpiration, had he feen as I
Her living charms with all the magic fraught
  Of thy more vivid fprings—reality !

My tafk is light to copy, not create,
  Were words but able to portray the grace,
And catch thofe beams of foul that animate
  The rapt expreffion of her angel face.

In each whofe change I feem to recognize
  The play of thought that caufes it, and fee
In the full meaning of her eloquent eyes
  The very foul and fource of poetry.

And if I now o'er Taſſo's pages throw
   A warmth, a colour, howſoever ſlight,
If through my pen Armida's beauties glow,
   However faintly, in his blaze of light:

Thine is the due whoſe lovelineſs and worth,
   Firſt touch'd my heart, and raiſed my ſoul
       above
The low and ſenſual deſires of earth,
   And gave foretaſte of heaven in thy love.

Caſtle Widenham.

THE GIRL AND THE BIRD.

THE night had fcarce her veil with-
    drawn,
  And ftars ftill mock'd the doubt-
    ful dawn,
    When up from where fhe lay
Sprang Mabel, heedlefs of the dark,
In her defire to hear the lark
    Salute the break of day.

Oft, oft fhe had been waken'd by,
When faft afleep, the joyous cry
    Of his familiar note:
But now awake, fhe fought the firft
Spontaneous, paffionate outburft
    Of his fleep-frefhen'd throat.

The vermeil tints now golden turning
Set nature's plaſtic features burning
　Beneath the ſun's fierce brow,
When, as if quicken'd by its flame,
From all the buſhes muſic came,
　A voice from every bough.

She liſtening at her lattice ſtood,
And ſaw from out the miſt-wreathed
　　　wood
　A thouſand ſongſters riſe ;
Some flutter'd up and quick reſumed
Their perch ; their pinions others plumed,
　As if to mount the ſkies.

But paſt the reſt, near out of ſight,
As ſcorning limits to his flight,
　The heavenly ſkylark ſoar'd ;
And as from earth he farther flew,
More weird and more unearthly grew
　The melody he pour'd.

In unifon her features play'd,
And reproduced each light and fhade
  Of his enraptured ftrain.
A new-born joy fhe feem'd to fnatch,
And, as it were, the madnefs catch
  Of his delirious brain.

Her frenzy heighten'd by the bird's,
Had fail'd by mere articulate words
  To paint delight fo ftrong.
As deep a meaning you could trace
In her expreffive, eloquent face
  As in the wild bird's fong.

TO —— ——.

THE autumn leaves are falling faft,
 The wind makes melancholy
   moan
  Among the beeches rudely blown
By dank November's blaft.

The fick fenefcence languifheth
 Of an effete expiring year,
 And faded are and grey and fere
The colours of its death,

Save where fome fiery creeper fhows
 In its enfanguined hectic bloom,
 The fever that foreruns its doom,
The taint that marks his clofe.

No more updrunken by the fun,
   But fwoln with rains which now are rife,
   The ftreams alone have larger life,
And with more riot run.

The infects born of fpring are dead,
   Nor of the birds that came with May
   Do any in our cold clime ftay,
But to the fouth have fled.

And with them thou—while I in lone
   And bitter folitude remain,
   And champ the curb, and fret the rein
That holds me here—thou gone.

And if at times I feem more gay,
   It is the better to conceal
   The utter lonelinefs I feel,
But would to none betray.

TO C. I. J.

THOUGH filent I, thefe flowers reveal
The fetting current of my thought,
And utter what I utterly feel,
      Forget-me-not!

Forget-me-not as years roll by,
But let it be my happy lot,
That thou refpondeft to the cry,
      Forget-me-not!

I carelefs if remember'd now,
Or if by abfent friends forgot,
My only care, my prayer that thou,
      Forget-me-not!

Living I'll ever write this day,
However diftant be the fpot,
And when I'm dead thefe ftones will fay,
                    Forget-me-not!

Florence, May 6, 1860.

TO —— ——.

TIS hard to tell, when looking upon
    thee,
      Whether thou art more good or
      fair or wise.
Did ever mortal move so gracefully,
   Were ever seen such sympathetic eyes?
And when conversing on some favourite theme
   Thou addest knowledge to one's special lore
Amazed one is to find the subject teem
   With latent beauties unobserved before.
Then all those better works which will
    endure,
     When these extrinsic gifts have pass'd away—

To tend the fick, the needy, and the poor,
  To love thy neighbour, and thy God obey—
All thefe combine to render thee what no man
Has ever feen till now—a perfect woman.

Florence, 1878.

YE alderliefeſt Dublin hills!
   On leaving you my full heart fills,
     And fill mine eyes with tears,
    Ye conjure up a ſhadowy train
Of bygone pleaſure daſh'd with pain,
  And grave with falling years.

Ye are the ſame, but ah! how changed
Am I ſince as a boy I ranged
  Your gorſe-fringed, fragrant ſlopes,
Ere able to diſtinguiſh truth
Amid the blinding fumes of youth,
  And youth's fallacious hopes.

But now I see with other eyes,
And though the mist that on them lies
   The visual sense obscure,
Still through the insight of the mind,
No more from clouds of error blind,
   Perception is more sure.

I see the changes wrought by time
Upon green youth and golden prime,
   And feel—myself grown old—
How small the chance that on this earth,
The loving pair who gave me birth
   I shall again behold.

Still let us hope,—this short life past,—
That we shall haply meet at last,
   To part no more in heaven,
Where free from sorrow and from pain,
We shall eternal peace obtain,
   Forgiving and forgiven.

On board the " Ulster."

TO —— ——.

1876.

NOW comes that joyous feafon of the
    year,
    When in their emerald apparel clad,
    The woods re-echo with the wild
    bird's fong;
When the fifh fpring and grubs turn butter-
    flies,
And nature breathes forth univerfal love,
And all is hope and promife; when each flower,
Though of the fimpleft, cowflip, violet,
Or the pale primrofe, is inftinct with life
And flouts her flaunting fifters of July;
And if with many another lovely flower

F

You have been ſtricken down, God grant that
      you
Reap utterly the genial influence
And fulleſt power of vivifying May.
Its balmy breath brace up the unſtrung nerves,
Freſh force impart into the drooping frame,
And graft its roſes on the pallid cheek.
May grace and peace be multiplied in you!
God give you of the fatneſs of the earth,
And may He give you of the dew of heaven,
He who to glory calls us by His Chriſt.
And after that you have ſufferèd awhile
Perfeēt you, ſtrengthen, ſtabliſh, ſettle you.
And as at this boon ſeaſon we behold
New life and beauty in the inanimate world,
And know that ſave corn die it bides alone,
But if it die it bringeth forth much fruit,
So knowing that we muſt paſs from life to
      death,
May that belief confirm, increaſe our faith
In Him who died for us that we may live.

TO A FAVOURITE CANARY THAT
I TROD UPON.

Fontainebleau, 1860.

NO found did aye fo fweet appear,
Or fall fo welcome on mine ear,
    As that which now I heard.
Ah! how my fpirit did rejoice
To catch once more thy gentle voice,
    My alderliefeft bird!

Since I had deem'd were ever hufh'd
Thofe dulcet notes as almoft crufh'd
    Beneath my feet he lay,
Quick came and went his fluttering breath,
His eyelids clofed,—alas! of death
    He feem'd the guilelefs prey.

But that I thought it finful, I
Had pray'd to God thou might'st not die,
    Beloved as thou art;
On bended knee had fought in prayer
Relief againſt the keen deſpair
    That wrung me to the heart.

" Live, live, my darling little pet,
Live, live," I cried,—" nor leave me yet,
    Again thy bright eyes ope."
Mine own with blinding tears were dim
As piteouſly I gazed on him,
    Almoſt bereft of hope.

When lo ! he piped—not ſkylark's note
When ſtraining his mellifluous throat
    The dawn of day to greet,
Not nightingale in greenwood grove
When pouring forth his ſoul in love
    Was ever half ſo ſweet.

By warrior bold the clarion's ſtrain,
By thirſty traveller falling rain,
   By wave-toſt pilgrim ſhore,
By miſer piles of glittering wealth,
By patient gleams of coming health—
   Were never welcomed more.

Flutter again thy gladſome wing,
Thy top-knot ruffle,—ſing, dear, ſing,
   Thou ſhould'ſt not me refuſe,
For there are many friends on earth,
And many a thing of greater worth,
   That I would liefer loſe.

"

L

M

As

When

When

T

Not nigh

When po

Was

VERONA.

THE moon is up, and not a fingle cloud
Floats in heaven's fapphire vault—the bufy world,
With all its fober, unromantic truths,
Is veil'd behind yon curtain, star-inwrought,
Which, as a drop fcene on the mimic ftage,
Appears to fall from heaven, and for awhile
Shut out appearance of profaic faĉt.
Abftraĉted thus from dull realities,
Fond fancy foars upon unfetter'd wing,
And, of the prefent heedlefs, views the paft
Through the rofe medium wrought by poetry.

And on what fpot of more poetic drift
Could fhe her vifion ope? Here ftill fhe fees
The enamour'd Juliet, on yon balcony,
Hang o'er the mufic of her Romeo;
Still hears the falfe and fickle Proteus
Sigh as he fings, "Ah! where is Sylvia?"
While on this fquare, by fhadows myftified,
His deathlefs fpirit ftalks. For it was here
Great Can received the greater Florentine,
And Dante's fpirit makes it hallow'd ground.
For if there's aught of poor mortality
That feems to fcape the common doom of
        death,
And ftill retain its old vitality,
'Tis the ethereal effence that furvives
In the rapt numbers of undying fong,
Which can with more religious influence,
Than mitred prelate in empurpled robe
Sublime and confecrate the meaneft fpot.
'Tis not, if we had power to raife the dead,
And converfe hold with the illuftrious paft,
An Alexander or Napoleon

That we would summon from the silent grave,
But Shakespeare, Dante, or the bard who sung
Of freed Jerusalem.   The warrior's fame
Were dead, not living through the poet's
      verse.

I must to bed—to dream, but not to sleep.

Verona, 1861.

VENICE.

AST night I had a ftrange, unearthly dream :
Methought I enter'd a vaft city, where
The ftreets were water, and I lay reclined
In an enchanted bark—nor knew I how
It floated ever onward, fince naught feem'd
To give it motion in its errant courfe,
And all was ftill and filent as the grave.
The glaffy bed on which the fhallop fwam
Was not a river, but more like the fea,
And dead fave where it fhimmer'd into life
Beneath the unclouded moon.   No banks were there,

But on each fide rofe up huge palaces,
Their portals level with the watery way.
Some maffive piles as if by giants built,
Others light, airy ftructures, that appear'd
More like the weird creation of a dream.
Myfterious boats, with dufky trappings hung,
Paff'd and repaff'd, from out whofe fable
 depths
Sounds that belied their gloomy origin
Flafh'd on my ftartled ears. Anon I faw
An open fpace by myriad lamps illumed,
O'er which a turret threw its ftately fhade.
Two fides were lined by marble palaces,
And on the third a gorgeous edifice,
Rich with barbaric gold and painted walls,
And fretted work and heaven-afpiring domes,
On countlefs columns bafed and crown'd with
 fpires,
Loom'd indiftinctly 'gainft the ftarry fky.
Then down a ftream fcarce broader than the
 boat,
Beneath innumerable bridges, I

Turn'd, through thick maſſes of ſuſpicious
    ſhade.
One bridge there was that tower'd above the
    reſt,
And ſpann'd two beetling blocks, on paſſing
    which
Deep ſighs and ghaſtly wailings froze my
    pulſe.
We then plunged into gloom more deep and
    denſe.

    *   *   *   *   *

Next morn I woke, and found myſelf in
    Venice.

Venice, 1861.

SPEZZIA.

HOW beautiful this morn! The
filver moon
Still rides in heaven as lady para-
mount,
Surrounded by a galaxy of ftars.
But at each moment pales her waning charms
Before the fplendour of the waking fun,
Who, in a robe of faffron-tinted fheen,
Forefhows his pompous advent. Maffa's
peaks
Are ftill conceal'd by overhanging clouds,
Which, like a load of care, appear t'opprefs
The hills' ambition with a leaden weight.
Still, ftill he lingers, as if loth to chafe

His unobtrufive rival from her throne,
Who pale and paler every moment grows,
Looking like maiden after midnight ball.
The eaft begins to glow, and to the fouth
Light, airy cloudlets float—pink, purple, grey.
More vivid now light flafhes all around,
Vermilion now, now orange it becomes.
The Tyrrhene coast, Gorgona's ifle appear.
The clouds grow crimfon, the blue vault more
       blue,
Till in a blaze of unendurable light
Burfts forth the full effulgence of the day.

La Spezzia, 1861.

TO —— ——.

I N youth's heyday, when vivid fancy
teems
With high-wrought vifions of
ideal blifs,
I never imaged in my wildeft dreams
A fpot fo beautiful, fo bright as this.

And fain would I now trace, for thy dear
fake,
The varied charms of its umbrageous fhore ;
Defcribe the calm of its tranflucent lake,
Unruffled even by the fifher's oar.

Since, though to fight so fair its furface dawns,
   No erring bark its treacherous bofom
      cleaves ;
For in the midft of it a whirlpool yawns,
   That fucks all down, and not a veftige
      leaves.

Yet mirror'd in its glafly face is feen
   The fairy fretwork of Gandolpho's towers,
And mellow'd into fofter, rarer green
   Its terraced gardens and o'erhanging
      bowers.

There Palazolo's white-wall'd convent ftands,
   And o'er it topples Monte Cavo's wood,
And clofe beneath the monaftery's lands
   Th' hiftoric fite where Alba Longa ftood.

Thefe the enchantments that my mufe infpire,
   Far from the bufy world and haunts of
      men,

And yet how faint this sketch—such scenes
    require
The painter's pencil, not the poet's pen.

I feel how powerless are words to trace
    The slightest semblance of this magic scene;
Yet time can ne'er its loveliness efface,
    Or from my heart its living memory
        wean.

And how describe the iris' violet wing,
    Or neighbouring pines that hang like clouds
        in air,
Which now with throstle's joyous music ring,
    Now echo back the nightingale's despair.

Lost mid the concert of the feather'd choir,
    Mid buzz of bees and gadding insects'
        hum,
I cannot clothe my thoughts as I desire—
    Mid nature's melody my voice is dumb.

But hark! for vefpers Palazolo ringing
   From his lone cell each cowl'd Francifcan
     woos,
And fee, the fun, its dying glory flinging,
   Has ftill for death referved its lovelieft
     hues.

Think, then, if abfent and alone, I fee
   So much to fill the heart and charm the
     eyes,
What were the rapture if enjoy'd with thee?
   This fpot were not then earth, but Paradife.

Albano, 1861.

H

GLENGARIFFE.

WOOD, water, mountain, what a
glorious fcene !
  Is that on which mine eyes tranf-
    ported hang !
The bay beneath, which but a few miles off
Is lafh'd to fury by the Atlantic waves
While meeting their ungovernable furge,
Sleeps like a mountain tarn.   Narciffus-like,
The emerald ifles peer in the cryftal deep,
As if to gaze on their own lovelinefs.
The fhore is fringed with birch, whofe afpen
    arms,
Fann'd by the breath of morn, wave trem-
    blingly,

And give as 'twere a movement to the lymph,
Unruffled elfe. Upon the northward flope
Of yonder mount the writhen thunderbolt
Seems to have left its trace, its jaggèd courfe
Being outlined there in ftone. Oh! what a
    fpot
To prompt the poet or philofopher!
For ev'n the latter, tracking nature's fprings,
Muft feek for large difcoveries in the mind.
We little know, in its unconfcious flight,
The fubtle part imagination plays.
What led Columbus to difcover worlds?
More fancy's impulfe than mechanic rule.
Here the rapt bard will meditating figh,
To find what faint idea he can give
Of fcene like this, which, though engraven
    deep
Upon the faithful tablet of the mind,
Yet feeks in vain a medium to convey
His fenfe of its weird beauty to the world.
Thou to be felt, Glengariffe, muft be feen.

  Glengariffe, 1860.

TO G. H.

BLINDING blaze of fummer
   bloom,
An odoriferous perfume,
As if on Saba's fhore diftill'd,
With utter light and fragrance fill'd
That garden—it was trimly kept,
And look'd as if by fairies fwept.
The flowers like ball-room beauties dreft,
Though of the lovely lovelieft,
Still in their rich apparel fhow'd
How much to art their nature owed.
I' the centre of an avenue,
Aloft a fpringing fountain threw

Fair water, in whofe plafhing fall
Was heard a found moft mufical—
A found exprefly form'd, 'twould feem,
To make thought-laden fancy dream.
The lady of this dainty place,
Which gains from her a living grace,
Comes daily here—they fay fhe can't
Abfent herfelf one day from Nant.
No wonder—for I here could ftay
And pafs, not hours, but life away,
Where art and nature fo unite
To charm the fenfe of fmell and fight,
And nothing lacks, fave certain eyes,
To make the place a Paradife.

Llyfdulas.

TO THE RIVER GUUL, NORWAY.

HOW sweet away from cities' strife,
To lead this simple, country life,
  And feel no more at school,
But free from the restraints of town,
And all its cares, to wander down
  The solitary Guul.

And what enchantment I rod in hand,
To fish its sparkling stream, and land
  A salmon from Flask pool;
The rise—the rush—the lightning run—
The leap—the struggle—until done
  He gasps beside the Guul.

Still fleeting are thefe joys, for foon
Will pafs this pleafant month of June,
  And fteal upon us Yule,
When frozen will its furface be,
And fcarce will trickle to the fea
  The once abounding Guul.

But memory of thefe calm delights,
Thefe halcyon days, thefe dreamlefs nights,
  Nor years nor clime can cool ;
As at this month, fo in December,
I'll drink to thee, as I remember
  Thy fummer golden Guul.

Bogen, 1869.

TO THE BRIDE—A RIVER.

OW happy I when at thy fide,
    Beautiful Bride!
      And though not mine thou art,
    Still thou forbiddeft not
That I fhould haunt the hallow'd fpot
    That fo enthralls my heart.

'Tis true, at times thou murmureft,
    As on thy breaft
    I caft my longing eyes,
And with keen expectation ftretch
Toward thee my eager arms, to catch
    Thy beauties as they rife.

Ah, yes! thrice happy 'tis to ſtray
    When lovely May
  Is opening out in all her pride,
And all her ſweets perfume the air,
  With one ſo innocent and fair
    As thou, belovèd Bride!

Creagh Caſtle.

WHAT is it sheds such magic o'er a
    name?
        And clothes the simplest with
        such wondrous spell?
What influence doth the wayward mind inflame,
    And makes it thus against itself rebel?

The name that once was like another, now
    Appears imbued with some resistless sway,
Or whence this sudden flush upon my brow,
    Why such emotion doth my heart betray?

Why doth my blood with such wild fever rush?
    Canst thou, Maria, tell the reason why
I never see thy name without a blush,
    I never hear it breathed without a sigh?

ON HEARING THAT A BEAUTIFUL GIRL WAS DYING, IF NOT DEAD, FROM SPASMS OF THE HEART.

WHAT! Florence ill!—I can't believe
 That fhe is fuffering, whom
I faw but only yefter eve,
 In beauty's brighteft bloom.

They only try to pierce my heart
 By telling me that death
Has fhot through hers an icy dart,
 That fhe now gafps for breath.

She in the heyday of her prime,
  The beautiful, the gay,
'Twere hard indeed before her time
  That fhe were fnatch'd away.

Who did where all were young and fair,
  Such admiration gain ?
Who moved with fuch a graceful air,
  Who fang like Florence Fane ?

How comes it then ?—perhaps the Lord
  Hath laid our idol low,
To chaften with avenging hand
  The friends that loved her fo.

And retribution thus imparts
  Her havoc to atone,
That fhe who broke fo many hearts,
  Should perifh through her own.

Ballyellis.

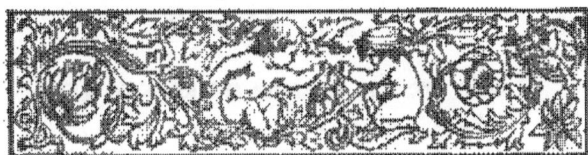

TO —— ——.

WHY afk thee for thy photograph
When in my heart it lies?
Heaven's brighteſt rays are not by
half
So graphic as thine eyes.

The funbeams when transferr'd by art
With them no funſhine bear,
The traits are like—but ah! we ſtart,
For life is wanting there.

Where are the lightnings of the eye,
The dimples on the cheek;
The bluſhes which though filently,
So eloquently ſpeak?

Thefe are the charms no art can give,
  No portraiture impart ;
Thefe, while its colours die, ftill live
  Undying in the heart.

TO —— ——.

SO fresh and passing fair thy face is,
So exquisite thy mien,
That in it all the several graces
Seem haply to convene.

Art uselessly her tribute lends
Fresh beauty to impart,
And shows how nature far transcends
The trickery of art.

Thy presence even hate disarms,
Thy sovran sway to prove,
As old admirers find new charms,
And seek again thy love.

The conftant hand outftretch'd to thee
  By fome rejected fwain,
But fhows how wrung the heart muft be
  That pleads and pleads in vain.

If thou art falfe my doom I know,
  My haplefs fate forefee,
The pain I feel for others' woe
  How paft all thought for me !

CUI PLACET OBLIVISCITUR, CUI DOLET MEMINIT.

WERE I like this grey dial-ftone,
 To count but funny hours,
The tafk how eafy in this lone,
 This gloomy world of ours!

For ev'n the moments of delight,
 I number here will pafs,
As fwift as fwallows in their flight,
 Or breath from looking-glafs.

The web of care exiftence weaves,
 Will banifh thefe from view;
And life, like autumn's yellow leaves,
 Affume a jaundiced hue.

K

The eagle walk inftarr'd with flowers,
   The terrace crown'd with limes,
The myrtle that triumphant towers
   In fpite of wintry rimes—

The glen of mafs, where holy men
   Were wont to offer prayer,
The haunted wood, the fairies' glen,
   As its inhabitants fair.

The ivied abbey, the old hall,
   The rufhing river's bend,
That laves its bafe, and, more than all,
   The welcome of a friend.

All, all will fade—regrets will mar
   Remembrance of this fpot ;
Our pleafures ne'er remember'd are,
   Our forrows ne'er forgot.

Ballynatray.

ADELINE.

'TWAS in the merry month of May,
When every bloſſom looks more
gay,
And every leaf more green ;
That in the woods of Inverawe,
Lord Walter for the firſt time faw
Young Adeline.

Upon the taſſell'd arches ſtood
Bright pearls of rain, and all the wood
Was ſilver'd with their ſheen,
When like a viſion of the night,
Upon his ſtartled, ſpell-bound ſight,
Flaſh'd Adeline.

Adown a funlit, flowery glade,
At times fhe tripp'd, at times delay'd,
　　Some firftling flower to glean ;
But not among them all was there
A flower fo fweet, fo frefh, fo fair
　　　　As Adeline.

They met—fhe liften'd—in her ear
He whifper'd words fhe blufh'd to hear,
　　And in that fylvan fcene
They often met—they often talk'd,
But once too oft with Walter walk'd
　　　　Loft Adeline !

The above and the two following pieces have been fet
to mufic by the author.

STANZAS FOR MUSIC.

WHEN ſhall we meet again?—the
      hour
   Has clang'd from yon green-
      mantled tower
  That parts us, Madelaine;
And as the echoes die away
They ſtrike a chord which ſeems to ſay,
  When ſhall we meet again?

When ſhall we meet again?—Perchance
For the laſt time thy earneſt glance
  Has pierced my aching brain,
And read the anſwer that deſpair
Imprints in living language there,
  When ſhall we meet again?

Few words are utter'd by the tongue,
When to its core the heart is wrung
  By agony of pain,
But now that honour bids me fly,
From out its depths escapes the cry,
  When shall we meet again?

The dreams of youth dissolve, and ope
Upon a dreary waste where hope
  Is dead, and where 'tis vain
From out the past one ray to steal,
Or ask the future to reveal,
  When we shall meet again.

STANZAS FOR MUSIC.

THEY told me I fhould not believe
    The words that Johnny fpoke,
  That he was given to deceive,
    And every promife broke;
They faid I would repent—regret—
I do—that I cannot forget.

My mother faid he was too poor
    To wed; when poverty
Show'd its gaunt vifage at the door,
    That love would quickly flee;
She ftopp'd my pleading by a threat—
I gave him up, but don't forget.

And often in the wakeful night,
   And in the dreamy day,
My Johnny flits before my fight :
   I cannot tear away
His image from my memory—yet
I ſtrive—I ſtruggle to forget.

The love implanted in my heart
   Has taken ſuch deep root,
That of myſelf it forms a part,
   And bears at times ſuch fruit,
That the ſweet 'gainſt the bitter ſet,
I would not if I could, forget.

TRANSLATIONS

TANTO GENTILE.

DANTE.

SO full of grace and modefty appears
   My liege, when fhe another doth
     falute,
    That not an eye to gaze upon her
dares,
And every tongue is from emotion mute.
Unmoved fhe hears her praife, and paffes on,
   Clad in the humble garb of modeft worth,
Looking a thing from heaven above come
    down,
   To fhow mankind a miracle on earth.
To all the world fhe doth fo pleafing feem,
   That through the eyes enthralment gains the
    heart,

Of which who have not felt it cannot dream,
   While from her lips, more fwift than Cupid's
         dart,
Seems a fweet fpirit full of love to fly,
Which the foul enters and there whifpers—figh.

DEL PELLEGRINI.

DANTE.

YE pilgrim guefts that through our
city ftray,
   And upon things not prefent
   meditate,
Come ye forfooth from countries far away,
   As your appearances would indicate?
Since as ye pafs along her ftreets, no tear
   Falls o'er the dolorous city from your eye,
Nor do ye, heedlefs, in the leaft appear
   To comprehend her grief's intenfity.
Could ye but ftay to hear the tale, my heart
   Affures me with an anfwering figh, that none

Would without weeping from her walls depart,
   Since from her, her own Beatrice is gone;
To tell whoſe merit in the fainteſt guiſe
Would as from ours draw tears from others'
   eyes.

VOI CHE ASCOLTATE.

PETRARCA.

YE that hear in thefe my fcatter'd
    rhymes
      The mournful fighs with which
      I fed my heart
In the early feafon of my youthful crimes,
   When other than from what I'm now in
     part;
Not only pardon do I hope to obtain,
   But ruth from thofe that love by fuffering
     know;
If in a ftyle fo varied I complain
   Of wild delufions and infenfate woe.

For now I ſee that to the world my name
   Has been a byword and a mockery,
Whence for myſelf I bluſh and feel deep ſhame,
   The bitter fruit of my idolatry,
With that clear knowledge through which now
     I deem
That the world's joys are but a ſhort-lived
   dream.

ERA IL GIORNO.

IT was that day on which the fun
grows black,
As if to mourn its Maker, that
I found
Myfelf, fair lady, taken all aback
By thy bright eyes, and in their trammels
bound.
Ill fuited feem'd the occafion for defence
Againft love's cruel and infidious blows,
So that I walk'd without fufpicion, whence
My fadnefs for the common grief arofe.
Love found me undefended 'gainft his fpears,
And faw a pathway open to the heart

M

Through eyes become an outlet but for tears;
  Still 'twas no honour, as I deem, to dart
Shafts againſt one unarmed, nor ev'n to ſhow,
Armed as he was from head to foot, his bow.

SON ANIMALI.

PETRARCA.

SOME animals there are of such
    strong sight,
    That the sun's noontide splen-
      dour they can bear;
Some blinded are by its exceffive light,
    Nor to go forth, except at evening, dare.
Others there are whose foolish wishes turn
    Them towards the sun, becaufe that it doth
      shine,
Who find it alfo has the power to burn.
    The latter cafe, alas! refembles mine;
For I'm not strong enough to endure the
    blaze

Of that fair ſun,—my liege,—nor know I
    how
In darkſome places to eſcape its rays,
    Since through theſe wet weak eyes, O
        Fortune! thou
Lead'ſt me to ſee the goal of my deſire;
Thus I purſue what ſets my ſoul on fire.

QUANTO PIU M' AVVICINO.

PETRARCA.

AS nearer I approach the final day
  That makes man's mifery of brief
  duration,
  More fwiftly I behold time pafs
away,
And that my truft in it is vain vexation.
Not long methinks fhall I be led aftray
 By love, fince fleeter than frefh-fallèn fnow
Diffolves this heavy load of cumbrous clay,
 Through which we have a refpite from our
 woe.
With death will thofe infenfate hopes expire
 That caufed me, mad-like, for fo long to rave,

And fears and laughter, and laments and ire ;
  And then a clearer infight we fhall have,
How oft by paths uncertain we advance,
How oft repine and figh through ignorance.

SOLO E PENSOSO.

PETRARCA.

ALONE and penfive through the
 fields I go,
  The defert fields, with flow and
  meafured pace,
Mine eyes intent to fhun the paths that fhow
 Of man's propinquity the flighteft trace :
No other means are left me in this need
 To fcape the fharp obfervance of my kin,
Who in thefe joylefs lineaments can read
 By my exterior how I burn within.
So that I fancy every hill and field
 And wood and river know the haplefs ftate

Of this my life, that is from man conceal'd.
　Still track I cannot find ſo deſolate,
But that Love ever at my ſide doth ſkim
With me converſing, as I do with him.

I'VO PIANGENDO.

PETRARCA.

I MOURN, I mourn, the bygone
　　years that I
　　In loving thing of mortal mould
　　have ſpent ;
Pinions I had, yet uſed them not to fly,
　To crawl ignobly on the ground content.
O King of heaven! eterne, inviſible,
　Which feeſt my wickedneſs, do not deny
To guide my erring thoughts when they rebel,
　And their defeƈt with heavenly grace ſupply,
That if I've lived in tempeſt and in ſtrife,
　I may in harbour and in quiet die ;

N

That glorious be the ending of my life,
   If its career was vain ; and, ah ! be nigh
To cheer what little yet remains to me.
Thou knoweft well—I hope alone in Thee !

SE LAMENTAR.

PETRARCA.

WHERE birds their melancholy
    defcant fing,
    And trees wave foftly in the
    fummer air ;
Where lucid water ripples murmuring—
  Heard from a frefh and flowery margent,
    where
I of love thinking, may fit down and write ;
  I fee, I hear, and underftand her whom
Heaven fhow'd but earth conceals : ev'n from
    that height
  Her fweet voice anfwers mine—" Ah ! why
    confume

Thyfelf before thy time ?" fhe foftly cries.
   " Why for the dead indulge a living flame,
Why pour a dolorous river from thine eyes ?
   Weep not for me, dear friend, my days
      became
Dying, eterne—and in eternal light,
When mine eyes feem'd to clofe, they gain'd
   new fight."

IN QUAL PARTE DEL CIEL.

PETRARCA.

WHERE in the heavens or in what
form below
Was found the idea from which
Nature took
That lovely face in which ſhe wiſh'd to ſhow
On earth the glimpſe of a celeſtial look:
Treſſes of gold ſo exquiſitely fine,
What goddeſs ever freed to ſummer's breath?
When did one heart ſuch excellence combine,
Although the prime one's guilty of my
death?
In vain he ſeeks for angel lovelineſs,
Who has not ſeen with what ſeductive lure

She turns her eloquent eyes; nor can he guefs
　How love is able both to kill and cure,
Who knows not with what fweet fighs fhe
　　　beguiles,
And how fhe fweetly fpeaks and fweetly fmiles!

LASSO CHE MAL ACCORTO.

PETRARCA.

ALAS! how unconfcious was I when love's flame
    Firft fear'd my bofom in that fatal hour,
And by degrees the tyrant lord became
    Of this my life, with full and fovran power.
I little deem'd with what perfiftent art
    It was enabled to pierce through, at length,
The ftubborn firmnefs of my harden'd heart.
    But fo fall thofe who overrate their ftrength.
Henceforth I know all remedy is vain,
    Other than this, my laft refource, to effay

If love will heed to man's entreaties deign;
    But prayers are vain, nor will I idly pray
That my heart may more meaſuredly reſpire,
But that ſhe feel ſome portion of its fire.

IO AMAI SEMPRE.

PETRARCA.

I EVER loved—nor yet from love
forbear ;
  Nay, I will love from day to day
  ſtill more,
That ſweet, ſweet ſpot where weeping I repair,
  Oft as love ravages my love-ſick core.
And I'm reſolved to love the time, the hour
  That all low thoughts within me has ſubdued,
And her the moſt whoſe angel face had power
  To win me by example to do good.
But who could thoſe dear foes, from every part,
  (Foes whom I cheriſh), aye expect to ſee

o

Together banded to affail my heart!
   Ah! with what forces, Love, thou conquereft
     me.
Yes—did not hope keep pace with my defire,
When I moft wifh to live, I fhould expire.

IO SON SI STANCO.

PETRARCA.

SO burden'd with the old accuftom'd
    load
    Of vicious habits and of fin am I,
    That I fear greatly fainting on the
road,
And falling captive to the enemy.
There came to fave me a great friend,—'tis true,
    With utter kindnefs, who did not remain ;
Since from my fight, fcarce feen, away he flew,
    And though I ftrive to fee him, it is vain.
But ftill his voice re-echoes in mine ear :
    O ye that travail, come, come unto me,

If others clofe it not, the way is clear.

What love, what favour, or what deftiny
Will furnifh me with wings, that, as a dove,
I may quit earth, and feek repofe above?

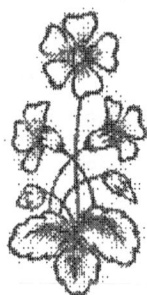

CESARE POI.

PETRARCA.

ESAR, what time the Egyptian
  traitor made
  Him prefent of his foeman's
  honour'd head,
To mafk the joy that o'er his features play'd,
 Diffembling, wept aloud,—as it is faid.
And Hannibal, when he beheld how Fate
 Againft the forely-ftricken empire turn'd,
His grim refentment to alleviate
 Laugh'd 'mid the maffes that around him
  mourn'd.
Thus does it happen that the mind conceals

Its every paſſion under falſe diſguiſe,
And ever oppoſite to what it feels.
      Hence if at times I ſing or ſmile, it is
Simply becauſe I know no other way
To hide the anguiſh I would not betray.

OR CHE IL CIELO.

PETRARCA.

NOW that the birds and beafts deep
    flumbering are,
      That winds are hufh'd, and ftill
      the earth and fky,
That round the heavens, Night wheels her
    filver car,
    And in their bed the wavelefs waters lie,—
I watch, I think, I burn, I weep,—for ftill
    Before me ftands the undoer of my peace.
My life's a war, nor does my poignant ill,
    Save when I think of my deftroyer, ceafe.
Thus from one clear and living fountain fpring

The ſweets and bitters upon which I feed ;
One hand there is that doth while healing ſting,
   Hence martyrdoms to martyrdoms ſucceed.
A thouſand times each day, I live, I die,
So far removed from a found ſtate am I.

LEVOMMI IL MIO PENSIER.

PETRARCA.

Y thoughts exalted me to regions where
　　She is I feek on earth, but find
　　no more,
And high in heaven, I beheld her,—fair,
　Much fairer, but lefs haughty than before.
Taking my hand, fhe whifper'd, "In this fphere,
　My wifhes granted, thou wilt join me yet;
I am fhe who troubled fo thy life's career,
　And pafſ'd my day before its fun had fet.
My blifs can't be conceived by mortal mind,
　I wait but thee, and what thou lovedſt fo,

P

My beauteous form, which is in earth infhrined."
    Why ceafe—why ope her hand, and let me
        go?
Since by thofe chafte, compaffionate accents
        fway'd,
But little wanted that in heaven I ftay'd.

CHI VUOL VEDER.

PETRARCA.

HO would behold what Nature can
    devife
    And Heaven create, fhould her
    contemplate who
Alone's a fun,—not folely in mine eyes,
  But in the purblind world's unheeding view.
Let him come foon, fince Death firft fteals the
    beft,
  And fuffers the moft criminal to ftay,
And this fair thing, expected by the bleft,
  Remains not here, but, mortal, flits away.
Here, if in time, he will each virtue fee,

Habits moſt noble, beauty exquiſite,
Knit in one frame with wondrous harmony.
  Then that I'm blinded from exceſs of light,
And that my verſe is voicelefs, he will ſay,
But will for ever weep, if he delay.

NE MAI PIETOSA MADRE.

PETRARCA.

TO her dear child, affectionate mother ne'er,
  Ne'er to her darling hufband, loving wife,
Gave with fuch tender, fuch folicitous care,
  Counfel fo faithful in the ftraits of life
As unto me that angel, who above,
  Beholding my fad exile here below,
Oft turns upon me her old look of love,
  Fraught with a twofold fympathy, as now
She with a mother's honeft warmth doth fear,
  Now with a lover's burns,—then fpeaking fhows

What things to ſhun, and what to follow here;
   Recounts our life's viciſſitudes and woes,
Then prays I ſoon may join her 'mid the bleſt,
Alone ſhe ſpeaking, have I peace or reſt.

ERANO I CAPEI D'ORO.

PETRARCA.

OOSE were her golden treſſes in the air,
Which toſſ'd them in diſorder in-
finite,
And from her luſtrous eyes, now ſeen ſo rare,
A radiance ſhone beyond all meaſure bright.
Her face (I know not if it truth expreſſ'd)
Fluſh'd with compaſſionate regard became,
Then with ſuch amorous touchwood in my
breaſt
What marvel that I burſt forth into flame?
Not as a mortal's did her gait appear,
No,—'twas an angel that I gazed upon;

An angel's voice, too, 'twas that rapt mine ear,
A heavenly fpirit, a quick, living fun,
Was fhe I faw,—if fhe be not fo now,
The wound ftill galls, although relax'd's the
    bow.

BENEDETTO SIA 'L GIORNO.

PETRARCA.

BLEST be the year, the month, the
    very day,
  The time, the feafon, the aufpicious
    hour,
The land, the fpot, where I firft felt the fway
Of two bright eyes that bound me in their
    power.
Bleft be the firft delicious tender woe
When fmit by Love I felt his poignant dart;
Bleft be the fatal arrows and the bow,
And the fweet wounds that pierced me to the
    heart;
Bleft the unnumber'd fair accounts that I,

Q

Calling my liege by name, have spread around;
Bleſt be the longing wiſh, the tear, the ſigh,
Bleſt every page in which ſhe lives renown'd
Through this my pen,—bleſt every thought
      and care
Which are but hers, in which none others ſhare.

ROTTA È L'ALTA COLONNA.

PETRARCA.

FALLEN is the column and the
    laurel tree
    Whose kindly shade refresh'd
    me when opprest,
Lost have I what I dare not hope to see
  In north and south, in farthest east or west.
Through death a double treasure I deplore
  That made me happy, confident, and bold,
Which neither earth nor empire can restore,
  Nor Oriental gem, nor power of gold.
But if this be the settled will of fate,
  What can I more in my affliction do

'Than downcaſt look, with eyes for ever wet?
  O life, which art ſo beautiful to view !
How eaſily in one morning diſappears
'The fruit acquired by moil of many years.

NON PUO FAR MORTE.

PETRARCA.

DEATH cannot make her faireft
    face unfair,
      But her fair face can lend a
        charm to death.
What need have I of other guidance there
    Than what her own example furnifheth ?
And He who was not mifer of His blood,
    And with bold foot burft through the gates
      of hell,
Seems by His dying to prove death a good.
    Come then, O death ! I like thy coming well,
And do not tarry, for the time has come,
    Though not in fact,—it really arrived

The hour my lady left her earthly home,
  Since which a ſingle day I have not lived ;
So bound in her's my life was, that my day
Was turn'd to night when Laura paſſ'd away.

VAGO AUGELLETTO.

PETRARCA.

DEAR little bird, that poureſt forth
    thy ſong,
    Or weepeſt mournfully time
    paſſ'd away,
Seeing that night and winter are ſo long,
  And all ſo diſtant the delights of May.
If, as thou feeleſt thy own miſery
  Thou knew'ſt how ſimilar my ſufferings were,
Thou wouldſt to this diſconſolate boſom fly,
  The dolorous anguiſh of my heart to ſhare.
I know not if our lots are like, ſince ſhe
  Thou mourneſt, it may be, is ſtill alive,

A fate begrudged by Heaven and Death to me.
   But now the feafon and fad hour revive
Remembrance of thofe fweet and bitter years,
And bid me feek thy fympathy with tears.

IN the fweet echoes that extracted
are
By thy fwift fingers from the
trembling chords,
Thou tell'ft of love in language clearer far
Than were attainable by fubtleft words.
Before fuch founds all dolorous vifions flee,
Like fhades before the fun, and as I ftill
Imbibe the magic of fuch melody,
Loft in enthralment is the force of will.
In itfelf perfect every note appears,
With a new fpirit of love's power replete,

R

When touch'd by thy dear hand—as moun-
    tain airs
  Are fill'd with fragrance frefher and more
    fweet,
If at morn ftraying through fome odorous
    bower
They brufh the uncover'd petal of a flower.

GLI OCCHI DI CH'IO.

PETRARCA.

THE eyes of which I once fo fondly
    fung,
      The arms, the hands, the feet,
      the lovely face
That me fo wholly from myfelf have wrung,
  And made fo unlike others of my race.
The wavy treffes of pure, lucent gold,
  The flafh of that angelic fmile, which made
Of earth a paradife, have now to cold
  Unfentient, immaterial duft decay'd.
And yet I live,—and, groping in the dark,
  Lament that light beloved fo much, fo long,

The tempest raging, pilotless my bark;
    Then hush'd for ever be my love-plumed
        song:
Spent is the fire that erst so fiercely burn'd,
And into mourning is my music turn'd.

SI SPESSO A CONSOLARMI.

SANAZZARO.

WEET sleep returns to comfort me
  so oft
   That almost I begin to wish for
   death,
Which is, perchance, more pleasing and more
  soft,
 And sweeter, too, than man imagineth;
For if the mind can understand and see
 When the dull limbs are languishing and
  dead,
And that more comforted I seem to be
 When from the body waking thought has
  fled,

Not vain my hope that when my ſoul at laſt
   Has burſt the bond of her terreſtrial chain,
She wake and ſee and her own pleaſures taſte.
   Rejoice then, ſoul, though vex'd by pre-
      ſent pain,
Since if on earth ſuch joy to thee is given,
What bliſs will thine be in thy native heaven!

MENTRE CHE' AMOR.

SANNAZARO.

WHILE love with fair ingenuous
    deceit,
   In its firſt fond deluſions nurſed
    my heart,
My mind, in verſe compaſſionate and ſweet,
   Sought its ſad tale of ſuffering to impart;
But when from year to year increaſed the ſtings,
   And from their lofty height the flowers fell
    down,
Driven from thoſe ſweet ſublime imaginings,
   Back on itſelf the conſcious mind was thrown;
Hence the ſhort courſe of mortal life I ſpend
   In lengthen'd ſilence and in utter ſhade,

Nor care for fame or other worldly end.
  Then, lady, ſeek ſome better, worthier aid,
A ſafer guide diſcover with thy wit,
  For I am worn, and waſted, and unfit.

COME CREDER DEBB'IO.

ARIOSTO.

OW can I deem, O Lord, that Thou
    wilt hear
        My cold and lifeleſs prayers, if
    while the voice
Cry for deliverance, Thou beholdeſt clear
    How in my bondage I at heart rejoice?
Do Thou who know'ſt the truth deliver me,
    Though my mad paſſions would the boon
        deny,
And, ah! ſend down Thy favour ſpeedily,
    Before I am doom'd a death of ſin to die.
Pardon my many ſins, O Lord eterne,
    And the foul habits which ſo blind mine eyes

3

That they can fcarcely good from ill difcern.

To fpare the penitent, man's province is,
But Thou, O Lord, alone canft drag from hell
Thofe who, lip-praying, ftill at heart rebel.

WRITTEN ON THE STATUE OF NIGHT,

BY MICHAEL ANGELO.

ROUGHT by an angel in this maſſy
ſtone
    Is Night, which in ſuch graceful
    poſe you ſee,
And, ſince ſhe ſleeps, has life, as here is ſhown :
    If doubtful, wake her,—ſhe will ſpeak to thee.

*Michael Angelo imperſonating the
ſtatue replies :*

Sweet is my ſleep, ſtill more of ſtone to be ;
    While ſhame and ſuffering exiſt below,
Thrice bleſt am I that cannot feel or ſee,
    So wake me not,—I prythee whiſper low.

POI CHE SDEGNO.

TRISSINO.

SINCE scorn has now unriveted the
    chain
    That Beauty forged and Love
      infidious wound,
And that comes back my liberty again
    From her whofe hand the links too tightly
      bound;
To its true good my fpirit would return,
    By madnefs erewhile driven for a thought
That caufed within my wayward heart to burn
    Ill-founded hopes, and pleafures which are
      naught.

That led by impulfe of more holy birth,
  I may perchance at that fair path arrive
Which difunites us from all thoughts of earth.
  And reafon which in me was fcarce alive,
But in another's impure keeping lay,
May take the reins and o'er the fenfes fway.

LIETA E CHIUSA.

BEMBO.

YE sweet secluded haunts to which I
fly,
Well pleased to shun the world
and live alone,
Who grudges me amid your shade to lie,
Now that so fervent the sun's rays have
grown ?
Seldom 'mid you I feel or grief or ire,
And ne'er so oft is fixed on heaven my sight,
Not elsewhere do my studies so inspire
Me with the wish to reach a higher flight.
The sweets of solitude ye taught to me,
From you I first learn'd how surpassing sweet

It is to feel from care and crosses free.

O stream beloved ! O well beloved retreat !
Would I could change this sea and esplanade
For your cool waters and refreshing shade.

PADRE ETERNO DEL CIEL.

VITTORIA COLONNA.

ETERNAL Father, with what grace,
    what love,
      What light, what varied kind-
        ness doft Thou free
Man from the world and from himfelf, and
    move
  His heart, that freely it return to Thee;
Return'd, thou warm'ft it with Thy quick'ning
    breath,
  And doft with knots the moft tenacious bind,
And clencheft it with fuch ftrong nails, that
    death
  Appears a living honour to the mind.

Thoughts fuch as thefe a fteadfaft faith infpire,
  Through which is light, and through light
    hope reveal'd,
And hope gives life to ftill fublimer fire,
  Whence to the foul the flefhly paffions yield,
Rebel no more,—nay, both together fly,
Of mortal cares difdainful, to the fky.

PARMI CHE'L SOL.

VITTORIA COLONNA.

THE fun, methinks, his wonted light
          denies,
     Lefs brilliant, too, his fifter's
          glories are,
I fee not wheeling through the ornate fkies
     Or friendly planet or refplendent ftar.
A heart with valour arm'd no more I fee,
     Fled is true honour, glory fair is fled,
And their companions, truth and chivalry.
     The trees are leaflefs and the flowrets dead,
Alone I fee wild waters and black air,
     The wind refrefhment gives not, nor fire heat,

All things on earth a different afpect wear
  Since Death my fun took to his dark retreat.
The courfe of nature in diforder lies,
Or truth is veil'd by forrow from mine eyes.

ORRIDA NOTTE.

L. TANSILLO.

HIDEOUS night, whose sable
  locks unbound,
    Beneath a veil of teeming dark-
      ness lie,
Come forth from thy dark caverns under-
    ground,
  And Nature's face in thy black colours dye.
I who have fretted at thy cold delay,
  Not less than from the fever I endure,
How I would praise thee if thou wouldst but
    stay,
  And me some sleep, ev'n for one night,
    procure!

I'd fay that thou cam'ft down from heaven,
    that thou
  Hadft myriad ftar-inwoven crowns, whofe
    light
Adorns the world; that to the wearied brow
  Thou gaveft reft, contentment, and delight.
In fhort, fo many fair things I would fay
That of fheer envy would expire the day.

DOGLIA CHE VAGA.

G. DELLA CASA.

TO that diftrefs which woman brings
the heart,
When wounding it with her
empiercing eyes,
No balm can Ida's dittany impart,
Nor lengthen'd weeping, nor defpairing cries.
Fly then from love,—they beft refift love's wiles
Who run leaft rifk in the unequal war;
When lovely woman fweetly fpeaks and fmiles,
Laments are prefent, death itfelf not far.
For with one look fair woman, when fhe wills,
Can lure the eye and rive the heart in twain.

Ah! monſtrous poiſon, that in pleaſing kills,
  Who knows of antidote to ſuch a bane!
Ah, no! the ſole correctives we poſſeſs
'Gainſt love, are abſence and forgetfulneſs.

MORMORANTI.

E. DI VALVASONE.

FRESH, hiftoric murmuring river,
 Clearer than any cryftal, and
  more pure,
 May Heaven for ever love you,
and for ever
From the fierce dog-ftar and his rage fecure.
On you, now rufhing lifelike through thefe
 rocks,
 Ah, may no tempeft fall, no harm defcend ;
May you unfullied or by fwain or flocks,
 From adverfe fate, benignant Heaven defend.
May your fair Naiads' loves meet happy end,
 May both your banks unfading verdure wear,

And every feafon fome frefh beauty lend
  To your tranflucent waters. Only bear
My image, whofe reflection they have caught,
  To her who tempers and controls my
    thought.

LA PRIGION FU.

F. COPPETTA.

SO fair the tomb was where the foul
    was laid
    And did fo forcibly the eyefight
    win,
That to regard the outfide others ftay'd,
  Regardlefs of the beauties hid within.
But fince with winter difappear'd the rofe,
  Since now the light of thofe bright eyes is
    feal'd,
The fpirit with refrefhen'd vigour fhows
  A thoufand treafures hitherto conceal'd.
There modefty and courtefy have place,
  Of other virtues, too, the facred quire

That man endows with fortitude and grace.
  Blind muſt they be who ſee and not admire.
Ah ! bleſt am I who, ſeeing this, far more
Than erſt I loved the body, now the ſoul
  adore.

LA BELLA PARGOLETTA.

TORQUATO TASSO.

THE girl who in her youth's firſt
flower
Has ne'er felt love within her
heart,
Nor heard from others of his power,
  Still with her lovely eyes will dart,
And all unconſcious ſmile,
  Nor knows what arms ſhe has the while.
Say, then, what fault with her be found,
  If men fall victims to thoſe arms
She never knew would wound?
  Oh, innocent and homicidal charms,
'Tis time that you by love were ſhown
What pain we ſuffer, in your own.

DIODATI.

MILTON.

I TELL thee, Diodati, with furprife,
    That I who erftwhile ridiculed
      the thought
      Of love, and did its ftratagems
  defpife,
  Am in its toils, like many another, caught.
Still, 'tis not vermeil cheek nor golden hair
  That dazzles me, or to whofe charms I bow ;
No—'tis the beauty of the heart, moft rare,
  A dignified deportment, and a brow
That with the light of lovely darknefs fhines,
  Difcourfe enrich'd with language more than
    one,

And fongs that from her ftar-encircled fhrines
　　Enabled were to draw the labouring moon,
And eyes, in which a fire fo eloquent glows
That of fmall ufe 'twould be the ears to clofe.

ANCH'IO. ·

MAGGI.

I TOO when fpring ran riot in my
        veins,
        Vaunted love's fever, which con-
        fumed me long,
And, telling to the mufe my darling pains,
    Made of my bitter plaints a honied fong.
But now that fober manhood fhows to me
    The fenfelefs folly of my youthful years,
And that more clearly their deceit I fee,
    My finging is converted into tears.
Repentance thus has led me to lament,
    And if youth's rapture was alloy'd with ills

My heart has now grown tranquil and content,
  Since forrow vivifies, while pleafure kills.
As mad enjoyments, though fo brief, deftroy,
So fage affliction leads to lafting joy.

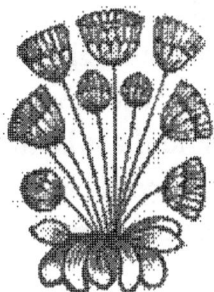

ITALIA! O ITALIA.

FILICAJA.

ITALY! O Italy! to whom
Fate moſt diſaſtrous beauty gave,
whence thou
Infinite ills inheriteſt; thy doom
Thou beareſt branded on thy ſorrowing brow.
Ah! hadſt thou been more ſtrong, or even leſs
fair,
Then would they fear thee more or love thee
leſs
Who by thy beauty ſeem conſumed, yet dare
Challenge to death the idol they careſs.
Then from the Alps I had not ſeen a flood
Of ſoldiers ſweep, or Gallic ſteeds daſh down

x

And drink, the Po encarnadined with blood;
 Nor ſeen thee, girt with weapons not thine
   own,
Aid at the hands of alien peoples crave,
Victor or vanquiſh'd, ſtill for ever ſlave!

OV' E ITALIA.

FILICAJA.

WHERE is thy own arm, Italy? Ah, why
    Employ another's? Thy de-
      fenders far
Surpafs thy offenders in ferocity ;
    Both were thy flaves, both now thy foemen
      are.
If't thus thou keep'ft the honour? is it thus
    Thou wouldft the glorious empire's fame
      preferve?
Thus towards that valour which was pledged
    to us,
    Our fathers' valour, thou wouldft faith
      obferve?

Away,—thy ancient ſtrength repudiate;
  Go,—ſleep and liſtleſs indolence eſpouſe,
'Mid blood, groans, ſhrieks, and perils ſtill more
     great.
  Sleep, vile Adultereſs! till the falchion rouſe
Thee from thy torpor, and, expoſed thy charms,
Thee ſlay beſotted in thy lover's arms.

DEATH, that tak'ft fo great a part
of me,
And leav'ft the other outfide thy
domain,
If what love is was ever felt by thee,
Or take this too, or give that back again.
But if thy fway fo far extendeth not,
Me with thy native ice at leaft endow,
And 'gainft the blows of my unhappy lot
Thou who offendedft fo, defend me now.
For neither power of herbs, nor magic art,
Nor reafon's balm fuffice to numb the
pain,

Or clofe the wounds of my afflicted heart,
    Whence to my natural forrow giving rein,
Weep, weep, I muft, and try my grief to affuage
By tracing her fair image on this page.

AURA SOAVE.

OFT breeze that toyeft fweetly with
the air,
And, wantoning amid the fhrubs
and flowers,
Firft gathereft the odours which they bear,
And then diffufeft them in fragrant fhowers:
O verdant meadow! O fair rufhing ftream,
Retreat moft grateful to my amorous fire,
That oft haft liften'd to the love-fick theme
Of hopes, and fears, and feverifh defire.
Henceforth thofe founds fo often heard by
you
I to an end, a very end would bring,

And much can will when ruled by reafon do.
  Still, if of her no more I weep or fing,
It cannot be I ever fhall forget
This verdant meadow and this rivulet.

GUARINI.

THIS mortal life, which feems fo fair,
    Is like a feather tempeft-toft,
    That favouring currents upward
        bear,
But which is in a moment loft.
Still if at times from earth it fpring
    In daring and adventurous flight,
And floats in air on outpoifed wing,
    It is becaufe its nature's light.
But foon in thoufand twifts and turns
To earth, fince being of earth, returns.

GUARINI.

AH, little bird! how very dear thou
      art,
         And how refembleft thy own
            fuffering
To the fad ftate of my enamour'd heart :
   Both captives are, and as thou fing'ft I fing.
Thou fing'ft to her whofe charms have fmitten
         thee,
   So, with this moft unfortunate difference, I
Sing, but to drown the pangs of memory ;
   In fong thou liveft, while I finging die.

GUARINI.

A ROSE Lycoris gave her flame,
    A rofe, methought, in Eden
        rear'd,
    And giving it fo red became
That fhe herfelf a rofe appear'd.
" Ah ! " falter'd Batto, with a figh
That did his heartfelt love difclofe,
" Unworthy, darling girl, am I
    To keep as gift the giving rofe ? "

———

Love, laughing, taunted rofe-crown'd May :
    "How foon your flowers' fweet fummer
        clofes ! "
But the fair Seafon anfwer'd :—" Say,
    Laft your joys longer than my rofes ? "

CHE FAR POTEA.

ZAPPI.

WHAT by herſelf could the ill-fated
  bride
  Of Collatino in ſuch danger do?
 She wept,—ſhe pray'd,—entreaties
vainly tried,
Vain were the tears that did her cheeks
 bedew.
Like falcon hanging o'er a dove, the ſword
 In menace o'er her ivory boſom flew,
But with none help or counſel to afford,
 What could the lonely, ill-ſtarr'd woman do?
She ſhould have died before ſhe ſinned, we
 know,
 But in herſelf how ſinn'd the fair, what time

She with her life's-blood ftain'd the dagger?
—No;
Alone Tarquinio perpetrated crime,
Againft—not with her. She was guilty too,
But only when her guiltlefs felf fhe flew.

THE LAST FAREWELL.

ZAPPI.

DEEP in my mind that night doth
    memory keep
    When home I left, and left my
    Mary there,
That dark, difaftrous night.—I faw her weep,
    Never lefs proud fhe was, nor aye more fair.
Oft, oft we faid "Farewell," again, " Farewell,"
    And where 'twas planted, there the foot
    remain'd ;
Oft, oft we parted, but the foot ftill fell
    On the fame fpot, although to part we feign'd.
The night at length is paft, the day appears,
    When in my extreme agony I faid,—

But what ſaid I, if floods of bitter tears
 All utterance choked ? I left, by blind fate
  ſped ;
But how left I ?—I cannot well aver,
 I only know I am no more with her.

DUE NINFE.

ZAPPI.

TWO maidens rivals were, in face
and fpeech,
    In power of fong, in motion, in
        repofe ;
And lovely fo that near the other each
    Star with a ftar appear'd, twin rofe with rofe.
'Twere hard to fay if this or that could bear
    The palm of beauty from her rival—you
Could truly fay none other is fo fair,
    But could not name the faireft of thefe two.
If fuch a couple had appear'd before
    The Idan fhepherd, not Cythæra's queen
In charm of face had gain'd the victory o'er

This peerlefs pair.   Which, then, had con-
queror been?
Either the apple Paris had divided,
Or the great conteft were ftill undecided.

CHI MI VEDE.

S. MAFFEI.

H E that beholds me with wan coun-
      tenance
    Walk through this foreſt ſlowly
    and alone,
And how from time to time, as in a trance,
    I rooted ſtand, like one transform'd to ſtone;
How oft I plunge into the blindeſt ways,
    The moſt impervious and the moſt profound;
How oft mine eyes that ſtream with tears I
    raiſe
    Up to the ſky, then caſt them on the
    ground:
" Ah! in what poignant anguiſh," he would ſay,
    " In what affliƈtion is that wretched man,

Who feems at times to breathe his foul away."
  Fool! thou but little knoweft how love can
The fenfes fteal, and fighs with fweets alloy;
I would not give my tears for all thy joy.

QUANDO LA FE.

CASAREGI.

WHEN my thoughts, plumed with
faith from fphere to fphere
Soar beyond heaven, O Lord,
before my fight
Thou doft amid Thy wingèd choirs appear
Within Thine own incomprehenfible light.
And if from thence to my own primal night
I turn with only reafon for my guide,
All tells of Thee and of Thy Image bright,
Which ev'n on earth in man is teftified;
I fee Thy Spirit, which infufes power
In earth's huge mafs, and caufes life to fpring

Within the grafs, the leaf, the fruit, the flower.
I fee Thee, borne on gentle breezes, wing
Thy way through air and water—yea, Thou art
Seen in all places fave my finful heart.

DONNA CHE BELLA SIA.

BONDI.

WOMAN that lovely is, nor steals
   Her charms from artificial aid;
   With docile mind, a heart that
     feels,
And manners sweet and nobly bred.
Not quick to love, or to be won,
   Whose sense and modesty despise—
Constant and true, content with one—
   Ev'n to seem fair in others' eyes.
"Find, piteous god," to Love I said,
   " Find me that girl, where'er she be ;
For I would love her,—nay, would wed."
   " If thou canst love aught else," cried he,
" Renounce thy plan, for such I ween
Was ne'er in my dominion seen."

IL SOGNO.

METASTASIO.

SHE whofe love my life endears,
 In fleep, at leaft, fometimes appears,
  To affuage my heart's fad ache.
  Ah, love! if fair and juft thou art,
To thefe fweet dreams more truth impart,
 Or never let me wake.

VITORELLI.

HEAVEN made us happy fathers
    defolate,
    Taking our daughters, modeft,
    wife, and fair.
For feeing each worthy of a nobler fate,
    Heaven fummon'd both from our paternal
    care.
From Hymen's brightly blazing torches, mine
    Death hurried to an early fepulchre
Within a convent's feal'd enclofure, thine
    Hath given herfelf eternal prifoner.
But thou, at leaft, art left fome little cheer,
    Since from the pafflefs portals of thy
    daughter

Thou canſt her gentle, pious accents hear,
  While blinded I by floods of bittereſt water
Ruſh to that marble where my angel lies,
And knock, and knock, and knock,—but none
  replies.

AFTER the ball-room's glare,
　　And fever, what delight
To breathe this balmy air,
　　And view the chaften'd light,
Which o'er the clear ferene
　　The fky's fair regent throws ;
How tranquil is the fcene,
　　What filence, what repofe!

No gadding zephyr breathes
　　Among the branching firs,
Amid the feftoon'd wreaths
　　Not even a leaflet ftirs :

The nightingale alone
  From bough to bough doth move,
And in a plaintive tone
  Calls to his abfent love.

She, ftartled at his cries,
  Quick as fhe can, draws near,
And lovingly replies,
  " Ah, weep not! I am here."
What tender troth they vow,
  Their fighs how foft they be ;
Why, Mary, wilt not thou
  Make fuch refponfe to me ?

QUANDO ELPIN.

F. ROMANI.

WHEN Elpin, weeping, perfeveres
　　To fupplicate thy love, thy ruth,
Place not too much belief in tears,
　For they but feldom tell the
　　truth.

With one benignant glance thou mayft
　Thy lover's martyrdom confole,
But let the glance thou giv'ft be chafte,
　His bold affurance to control.

It may be he requeſt a ſmile,
  One little ſmile do not deny ;
But let him ſee thee coy the while,
  Nor with another ſmile reply.

But if he ſhould a kiſs demand,
  One kiſs alone and nothing more ;
That, Roſe, with all thy ſtrength withſtand,
  The kiſs beſtow'd,—all, all is o'er.

Thou know'ſt not what fierce fire it wakes,
  What poiſon the ſweet lips convey,
It adds freſh force to him who takes,
  From her who gives takes all away.

When maiden yielding to its flames
  For the firſt time her love has kiſt,
" Give all the reſt," the heart exclaims,
  And ſhe's too feeble to reſiſt.

ALFIERI.

WHAT! here in this neglected tomb
      remain
      The bones of the great epic bard,
      who fole
Made the antique trump refound in modern
      ftrain,
      And echo through the world from pole to
      pole?
What!—Rome a monument to him deny
      Who foar'd to heaven upon immortal wings,
While here, in this your greateft temple, lie
      The wretched rabble of your bifhop-kings?
Ye fwarms of dead that never were alive,
      Arife! begone! and let the Vatican

Be purged from the foul fmells that ftill fur-
vive,
   And in its faireft midft be placed a man.
There were a fhrine fole worthy of the two,
To Taffo raifed by Michael Angelo.

SONNET AFFIXED TO THE PORTAL OF

ST. PETER'S, ROME.

March 10, 1861.

WHEN the pale judge to abject terror
            prey,
    To his propofal bade the mob
            reply,
In their black rancour unrelenting they
    Cried " Live Barabbas, and let Jefus die ! "
He died—borne down by the difgrace and
            pain,
    And was beholden hanging from the tree,
But the third day triumphant rofe again,
    Crown'd with the palms of his new victory.
Drunkards, perceiving not their fin's extent,

Pius ! prefer a robber unto thee,
And in their madnefs are moft confident.
But as God-man invincible thou'lt fee,
Phœnix-like rifing, at thy feet fall down
Him who now dares to fnatch away thy
crown.

THE lilies on Cogava's brink
    Tofs their fair heads on high,
    While low their fhadow-fifters fink,
    Of their own beauty fhy.
Ah! why as when a child, ah, why
    Can I not wet my fleeve with the certainty
Of gathering thofe which at the bottom lie?

The bird of fong in Naniva
Her home of plum-flowers forms,
But by her tears
Betrays her fears

Left they be fwept away
By defolating ftorms.
But to preferve unharm'd thofe flowers,
Could tender tears avail,
Doft think I'd weep lefs plenteous fhowers
Than thou, poor Nightingale!

———

Where is the realm of the wind,
The flowers' implacable foe?
For I would forth to encounter it.   But no,
Bleft rather are ye flowers that find
Death fweet, difperfe and difappear;
Man has on earth a long career,
But where's the thing, whatever be its fpan,
- Whofe end is half fo fad as that of man?

Florence, 1877.

CHISWICK PRESS:—C. WHITTINGHAM, TOOKS COURT,
CHANCERY LANE.